The Lazy Investors' Guide
Save money. Retire early. The lazy way.

By Michael Lund & Eric Dahl

© 2014

All rights reserved. No part of this publication may be reproduced, distributed, or transmitted in any form or by any means, including photocopying, recording, or other electronic or mechanical methods, without the prior written permission of the publisher, except in the case of brief quotations embodied in critical reviews and certain other noncommercial uses permitted by copyright law.

Disclaimer

This material has been prepared by The Lazy Investors (Michael Lund and Eric Dahl). This document is for information and educational purposes only, and does not purport to guarantee actual outcomes. It is not, and should not be construed as investment advice or as a recommendation regarding any particular strategy or investment instrument.

The opinions expressed in this document are based on our current opinions, and may be subject to change at any time without notification. Readers are free to disagree with the opinions expressed. Should any of the assumptions used in the document not materialize, then the outcomes assumed herein could vary substantially.

Readers should be aware that every investment entails risk. There is no guarantee that the investment strategies recommended will achieve the suggested results under every market condition, and each investor should evaluate his/her individual ability to invest using these strategies for a long term, especially during turbulent periods in the markets. The Company is not making any representation that the products and strategies discussed will achieve similar results as those discussed herein.

No part of this book may be reproduced in any manner, in part or in whole, without the prior written approval of The Lazy Investors.

The information contained herein is offered on the understanding that readers will form their own independent decisions regarding a course of action to be pursued, with in relation to any product or strategy discussed here. Such actions need to be considered appropriate based on a reader's own judgment, with full knowledge of the risks and benefits of their decisions.

The Lazy Investors shall not bear any liability for any losses or damages of any nature whatsoever, sustained by readers as a result of this material. You should consult a qualified financial (or other) advisor with respect to the suitability of acting on the information contained herein.

By accepting this material, you understand, acknowledge and accept everything stated above.

For more info and further readings, please visit us at
http://www.thelazyinvestors.com

PROLOGUE

"Because a thing seems difficult for you, do not think it is IMPOSSIBLE for anyone to accomplish" - **Marcus Aurelius**

WHAT'S ALL THE BUZZ ABOUT?

Be honest now: How many of you really don't look forward to going to those class reunions, office Christmas parties or ladies night out events anymore? There's always some guy or gal out there, who is constantly bragging about how well their investments have done, and what a killing they made - despite the recent financial crisis.

But each time you look at your financial statements, all you see are flat lines or a sea of red. And every time you talk to your broker, all you hear is:

"Don't worry...I've got a great trade lined up for you. It'll blow your mind away!"

Yea right! The only things blown away are your returns! You'd like to be like Mr./Ms. Loudmouth and learn all about "Buying Low and Selling High", "Market timing", "Reading the Charts". But you're too lazy (or smart!) to do all that nimble stuff:

- Too much market watching
- Lots of research
- Constantly waiting for "hot tips" to pan out

It's too stressful, and it takes lots of work involved. It just seems so impossible to do - right? Well...not really.

Today, we'll introduce you to a novel investment idea - called **"Lazy Investing"** - that'll give you an edge and revolutionize the way you invest. Seriously, guys and gals, if you really want to take control of your investments, then Lazy Investing can make that happen. How? By helping you relinquish some of that "control'!

Say what?

You see, unlike the more "traditional" investment styles, where investors are constantly buying, selling and trading stocks, the Lazy Investing approach takes a more laid back view to making money. Don't get the wrong idea:

<u>Lazy Investing is not about short cuts or cutting corners!</u>

In fact, Lazy Investing is deeply rooted in the science of investing and investor psychology. But unlike other investment philosophies, where you are constantly watching stock tickers and trading screens, Lazy Investing is a more "carefree" way for YOU (and not your Broker or Financial Advisor) to make money.

WHAT'S IN STORE FOR YOU?

Actually, we've got a lot lined up for you between the pages of this book on Lazy Investing:

- You'll learn why investing today is such a scary thought, and what's driving investors to stay on the sidelines with their money invested in low return vehicles
- We'll reveal some popular Myths about the stock market, and expose them as being just that - "myths" that prevent YOU from making money in stocks
- We'll explore why this whole concept of Lazy Investing is catching fire all around the globe
- We'll introduce you to what Lazy Investing is all about
- You'll get to see, up close, some great examples of Lazy Investing building blocks
- Together, we'll also see what some of those Lazy Investing building blocks can and can't do for your portfolio

- We'll walk you through the decision making process of whether Lazy Investing is *really* right for you
- And last, but certainly not least, you'll get an inside look at the Ultimate Lazy Investors Portfolio - several versions of them actually!

But that's not all you learn. We know the reason you are reading this book is because you are too lazy (or smart, we'd say) to try and do this all by yourself. Investing doesn't have to be as difficult as it's usually made out to be. There's got to be an easier way to do it right, with minimal effort, and end up ahead in the race. Investing has got to be less about paying fees to others (Brokers and Advisors), and more about paying YOURSELF.

And we couldn't agree more.

So we've put together a "Lazy Investors Toolbox" for you at the end of the book. You'll find some excellent checklists and questionnaires that you can use to define, refine and improve your personal Lazy investment style and Lazy Portfolio.

Take it from someone who knows: By the time you've read through this entire book, you'll be aching to go back to those gatherings and yell back at Mr./Ms. Loudmouth and say to them:

"In your face...Loudmouth!"

Happy Lazy Investing to you all!

INTRODUCTION

"Beware of geeks bearing formulas" - **Warren Buffett**

WHY BE LAZY?

The world is a much busier place today than it was in the late 1920's. Thanks to technology, the average individual is multi-tasking and doing so many things at once, that it is often easy to drop the ball on some important things - like staying on top of your stock picks and investments.

While forgetting to pick up the dry cleaning or missing a drink date with Marry and Joe might not be all that bad, not selling an investment at the right time, or buying one when the price isn't just right, can be very costly indeed. In fact, in some cases, your entire retirement portfolio can be completely wiped out if you (or your stock broker) aren't on the ball all the time.

- But who wants their lives to revolve around the stock markets?
- Which of us would rather execute a trade than sit with Marry and Joe and enjoy a margarita (It's their turn to pick up the tab anyway!)?
- How many of us have the wherewithal to understand "shorts" and "tops" and "bottoms" and "supports" and "resistance" anyway?

If you feel this is you we are talking about, then you are not alone. Millions of individuals around the globe are with you, and all of them have decided that, rather than live to invest, they'd rather invest in living. Instead of losing sleep over their investments, they are embracing the lazy route to investing.

PUTTING STOCK IN STOCK MARKETS - A SCARY THOUGHT!

Stock markets are a scary place to be in right now - especially if you are not a constant "market watcher". Sure, the volatility of the markets can truly be a friend to nimble traders. But for most average, "every day", lazy types, volatility can be devastating. That's because most guys and gals have day jobs - so they can earn enough to have something to invest. Most of us don't have the luxury of taking advantage of that volatility like the "geeks" can.

And if you've been watching the ups and downs on the Dow Jones Industrial Average (DJIA), The S&P 500 or the NASDAQ over the recent past, you're probably already sick to your stomach. For all you lazy investors out there, at least there's some good news: Misery loves company, and you're not alone!

But guess what folks? Volatility isn't just a thing of today. Back in 2000, when the "geeks" were predicting everyone would cash in on the Tech Boom - guess what happened? The infamous Tech Bubble burst! And as many will recall, there was blood in the markets, and a lot of Baby Boomers are still licking their wounds today.

And when we look even further back, we still find evidence that - if not handled correctly - stock markets can indeed be scary places. Despite all the talk of "sure things" and "unbeatable formulas" even back then, many investors felt the pain of losing it all during the infamous stock market crash of 1928-29.

Whether there is pattern to observe in the charts, or absurdity in its interpretation, it sure seems like déjà vu - doesn't it? Well, only time will tell. But the scary signals keep erupting almost every day, and that's scaring investors into tucking their savings under the mattress, pulling the blankets over their heads - and hoping this too will pass. And rightly so, but in the meantime, they are missing out on some great investment opportunities.

YOU CAN'T TIME THE MARKET (...AND WIN!)

As the chart above shows, there is eerie similarity to the markets' behaviour today when compared to 1928-29. Yet (not surprisingly...) the same Pundits and Gurus of yesteryears, who made their fortunes selling "secret formulas" for beating the market, are at it again today. And if you are once bitten, twice shy, you'll be very wary of biting hook, line and sinker again.

The geeks who come bearing formulas to beat the market will assure you that you can indeed beat the market. "Just one trade...IN and OUT...that's all!" is a line that usually gets you. But market watchers and historians will tell you:

"You can't beat the market by trying to time it!"

Just think about it for a minute, folks: If that weren't true, then everyone that wrote books like "How To Time The Market And Score Big!" or "Get Rich By Timing The Market!", wouldn't really have had to write those books, now would they? They would be happily retired on the proceeds of their market-timing investments, never having to worry about collecting dimes on book royalties.

You see, "timing" entails waiting on the sidelines with bags of investible cash, and then jumping in and out of the market at just the "right time" to cash out big. Market timing is like a precision Special Ops mission: You scope out the markets. You execute your plan. You sit back and count your winnings. Usually, all this happens in a matter of days/weeks, not many years as conventional investment wisdom dictates.

But here's the FACT: That strategy just doesn't work. And here's why:

Despite what the formula-spinning geeks tell you, as the data below shows, being out of the market (staying on the sidelines with your precious bag of cash, waiting for the right time to get in) on just 10 good days over a 10-year period (2002 to 2012), would have eroded your nest egg by 4.64%. It gets worse: -32.19% and almost -50% if you missed out on 20 best days or 30 great market days respectively.

None of those timing formulas really tell you which days those will be - they can't! So while you waited on the sidelines, others that were fully invested (over that same 10 year period) made the killing - up by almost 70%.

Now how cool would you feel telling THAT to Mr./Ms. Loudmouth!

UNDERSTANDING STOCK MARKET MYTHS

So now that we've set the record straight about formula-selling geeks, we might as well go about bursting some other popular myths about the stock market. If we want to convince you that you really CAN make money in the markets, then we need to also tell you how you definitely WON'T do so. The intention here is not to scare you out of the stock market, but instead to scare you into staying *in* it - but with the right attitude: The Lazy Investors' Attitude.

i) Myth #1: Anyone can make money in stocks:

This one is partially true - but only with a few important caveats: You need to invest according to your psychology. You need to understand your investments. And you need to be disciplined in your investment methodology.

Most every-day Joe's and Jane's are not traders who keep their eyes glued to stock trading screens. For the vast majority of us, we prefer far easier ways to making money in stocks. And that requires a more laid back approach - The Lazy way and NOT the trading way!

ii) Myth #2: Listen to a Guru:

WRONG...Wrong...Utterly Wrong! The mere fact that these so called "Gurus" are still out there is because their "formulas" just don't work. Historical data proves that. And since they haven't yet made enough money selling their "secrets", they keep repackaging those same stale secrets - year after year - and offering them as "new and improved formulas".

Listen up, folks! The proof is in the pudding, so to speak. The only way to make money in the stock market is to understand what goes into a "formula", and only use it if it makes sense to you.

Unfortunately, a vast majority of the Guru-formulas fail that test miserably. What they are selling just won't work for investors who don't understand market timing, volatility, Candlestick charts and Moving Averages. We are just too lazy to take time to understand them. Nor should we! Give me something simple any day, and I'll embrace it in a heartbeat. Wouldn't you?

iii) Myth #3: Stock Markets are like Casinos:

Wrong! As we've seen above (through historical data points), nothing could be further from gambling than disciplined investing in the stock market.

Of course, if you are into "market timing" or "making a quick buck", then you are definitely rolling the dice with your retirement nest egg. And therein lies the problem: Because most investment ideas out there are so complex, everyday-Joe and ordinary-Jane end up rolling the dice.

Making investment simple, less complicated and laid back, is the only way to ensure ordinary investors make REAL money in stocks. And that's exactly what Lazy Investing is all about.

iv) Myth #4: "The more stocks you hold, the quicker you'll make a fortune!":

Wow...and how much would we have to invest in each of those thousands of stocks? This is such a fallacy that talking about it at cocktail parties will just make you the laughing stock of the event!

There is such a thing as "over diversification". Like many things in life, making money in investments doesn't require "quantity". It's all about "quality". Profiting from investing takes time, no matter how brilliant or extraordinary you may think your investment skills are!

Investing in too many stocks, bonds, ETFs, Index Funds and Mutual Funds, can lead to your investment Portfolio being too unwieldy. The "I'll take one of each" investment strategy doesn't really work, and could even work at cross-purposes to your overall portfolio building strategy.

v) Myth #5: "It's a good company...invest in it!":

Bad idea! While many good companies make great investments, it's not necessarily so. Wall Street is littered with the bodies of good companies that made their shareholders go bust! Remember Enron, WorldCom, Washington Mutual and Lehman Brothers?

Well, folks, all of these were excellent companies (in fact Enron was dubbed the "darling of Wall Street" at one point!) to begin with, but turned out to be lousy investments. The moral of the story here is:

Be very careful about picking individual stocks of companies. You never know what lies underneath!

SO, YOU STILL THINK YOU CAN BEAT THE MARKET?

Hmm....come on now, haven't you been paying attention? IT JUST CAN'T BE DONE! Not even by the so-called "experts". You may do it a couple of times in 10 years, but you'll be so far underwater with your investments by then, that come time to retire, you'll be in the poor house.

Still don't get it, do you?

Well, let's do some math then, shall we?

Let's say Jill is gung-ho to beat the market. She gets a hot tip from her broker about 3 stocks that are a "sure thing". So, she ploughs $3,000 into the market, investing $1,000 into each of the stocks.

Let's assume that her broker charges her $10 per trade - to initially buy the stocks, and then to sell them when the time is right. Well, here's what this "formula" looks like:

- Even before Jill sees a dime in profits, she can count on being $60 out of pocket - regardless of whether the market moves up or down!
- Jill has already spent 2% of her investment on commissions (in many cases there will be additional costs involved - e.g. Electronic Exchange fees, Taxes etc.)!
- In order to break even, her $3,000 investments must go up to $3,060!
- And for Jill to reach her Target rate of return (5%), her investments must rise by a whopping minimum 7% (5% target PLUS 2% paid in commissions)!

Given that most market timers say that "you'll be in and out in a matter of days!", how likely is it that Jill will make a 7% return on her investment in just days? Well, if Jill is a betting lady, she may favor the odds, but most sane investors just wouldn't!

If the Fees and Commissions are slightly higher (say 3% for example), or if the market dips for several sessions after Jill times her entry, she could be in for a real surprise - and a very unpleasant one at that! She could be stuck with those investments for a very long time. Worst-case scenario, she may be forced to sell at a loss, losing 2% at minimum.

Maybe that'll convince you to never believe geeks bearing formulas!

SO, WHAT'S THE ANSWER?

It's simple! Be smart as a Lazy Investor, and don't get fooled by the formula touting geeks. Here's a secret, folks: Money CAN be made in stocks. But the aim is for YOU to be making it, and not your Broker or Financial Advisor. And that's the sole objective of Lazy Investing. To make you money, to protect your money, to grow your money, with the smallest effort necessary.

In the sections to follow, we'll take a closer look at what Lazy Investing means, and how anyone with a Lazy mentality can make REAL money in the stock market. And as you go through everything that you read here, remember the following:

- This book is NOT about advocating a specific investment product
- It is NOT about telling you where to invest and how much to invest
- And neither is it about giving you "get rich quick" advice

What this book IS about is: Helping you understand that investing successfully is all about long-term, disciplined deployment of your savings, and NOT about gambling it away in quick trading strategies that don't work.

What this book IS about is: Helping you believe that you don't need to actively monitor and manage your investments on an hour-by-hour, day-to-day basis. We'll teach you how you can be lazy about your investments, and still end up ahead of all the trading-types you meet every day!

WHAT IS LAZY INVESTING?

"Time is your friend; impulse is your enemy"
- Jack Bogle (ex CEO & Founder of Vanguard)

Whew...you made it past all the boring stuff. Good for you! From here on, we're about to explore the meat and potatoes of Lazy Investing. The ideas, the methods, the means. But before we dive into the nuts and bolts, let me ask you something:

How many of you have heard the story of the Turtle and the Hare? No matter how it's changed over the years, and regardless of who the characters are made to fill in for (depending on which time period the story is made to depict), the slow moving, steady-Eddy, non-sexy, lazy Turtle always wins. In fact, the nimble, fast moving, quick acting Hare is always left more than a country mile behind, eating the Turtle's dust. So it is with Lazy Investing. Slow and steady definitely wins the money race.

a) The Basics

All right, for those of you who want a short answer to the question: "What is Lazy Investing?", the answer is right there in that age old tale about the lazy turtle and the hyper-fast hare. The main difference between that story and the Lazy investment thesis is in how the race is won. For Lazy Investors, success isn't about sprinting down a racetrack. It comes from:

- Having a long-term view of your investments
- Resisting the temptation of moving in and out of stocks to capitalize on volatility
- Investing in, rather than trading off, the stock market

Investors come in two basic flavors: Active (like the Hare) and Passive (like the Turtle). So before we dive any further into the world of the Lazy Investor, let's take a closer look at these two types of investors.

i) A flare for activity:

Active investment managers are those that are constantly monitoring, always making moves, and actively changing investments to address a dynamically fluid investment climate. They are paid to do so, often times by unsuspecting investors like you and I.

- Like the Hare, they sprint up and down their investing horizon, looking for opportunities to nibble at
- They try to buy investment vehicles when they believe the price is just right
- They'll quickly sell off investments they feel are not performing as expected

And they do this over, and over, and over, in the hope that they can beat the returns of their peers and industry benchmarks. And just as any activity of our bodies burns calories, so too does activity in our investment burn returns. Since pictures really can say a thousand words, let's paint a picture of what we've just learned here:

The "cost" for actively managed portfolios comes in various forms:
- Management Expense Ratio (MERs)
- Management Fees
- Trading Fees
- Commissions
- Loads

While some of these costs are paid annually, based on the balance of your portfolio (regardless of whether your portfolio balance increased or declined during the year!), others are paid each time an activity (Buy, Sell, Transfer) takes place in the portfolio. As is evident from the long-term investment graph above, clearly a "no cost" investment does much better than one that costs 0.25%, which fares far better than one that costs 0.90%!

So what does this mean in terms of how much of their portfolios investor's give away to active managers? Well, since pictures are your thing, let's paint you yet another (scary!) picture:

Assuming that the Active Manager has a 1.25% expense ratio, and further assuming he/she returns 5% regularly, year, over year...over year, for 10 consecutive years, you'll have handed **just over 30% of your returns** to him/her over that period. Sounds reasonable to you, does it?

Hmm...what if you knew that in 25 years, roughly **38% of your returns would be eroded** through these charges, and within 50 years **your "manager" will be earning more** on your portfolio (51%) that you do. And that's just in MER - we haven't even factored other costs like Trading Fees and Commissions yet!

The bottom line is, most Active Managers don't even manage to **consistently beat** their peers and industry benchmarks over a long term. A few good years make them look like "Gurus", but most of the time they can't even manage that. And yet, regardless of whether your portfolio wins or loses, you still pay them to actively manage your portfolio.

"Wow...that's scary!", I hear you say. That's really putting it mildly. In some circles one would call it downright unfair...or crazy. We vote for the latter.

ii) Passively successful:

By contrast, Lazy investing is more passive in nature - like the Turtle, slow and steady, always winning. The object of Lazy investing is not about actively trying to beat a benchmark. Instead, most Lazy investment products are structurally designed to mimic (or follow) the benchmark. So, at the end of the day, since active managers aren't likely to consistently beat a benchmark anyway, why pay them for trying?

- Lazy investors don't believe in heavy trading
- Their investments aren't designed to continually move in and out of the market
- They are designed to win through slow-and-steady, sustained jogging, as opposed to risky short sprints that leave you breathless
- They are built to "flow with the tide", and not risk swimming against fast moving waters

But most of all:

- Lazy Investments cost just a fraction of Actively Managed products!

By passively embracing the benchmark, Lazy investment tools will deliver returns in terms of whatever the prevailing market sentiment is. Why try beating a benchmark when there is a preponderance of evidence to show it cannot be consistently done, year-in and year-out?

And that, more than anything else, helps the Lazy Turtle get ahead of the Active Hare in the investment game.

b) Examples Of Lazy Investing

Okay, then. Now that we have a pretty good idea of what Lazy Investing means, it's time for us to take a closer look at some examples of "Lazy products" out there.

The world of investing has come a long way since the 1928-29 and the 2000 market crashes. New and innovative products have sprung up that appeal to every style, taste and temperament of investor. As a matter of fact, there are so many flavors of the same product that sometimes the average investor feels overwhelmed with choice.

So let's try and make sense of it all, shall we?

In a book of the type that you are reading, it's hard (rather, impossible!) to cover each and every investment tool available. Newer and more complex ones are always on the horizon, just as older ones are pulled off the shelves. So what we're about to take a look at are some common tools that a Lazy Investor should have in his/her Toolbox.

i) Mutual Funds:

This Mother-of-All-Investment vehicle's is so popular that there's not much new that we can add to the discussion. However, since we are talking "Lazy", we'll keep our discussions focused on how, despite their relatively high-cost structure, Mutual Funds can be used to build (at least partially) a Lazy Portfolio. And today, thanks to the tremendous competition amongst Mutual Fund sponsoring companies, the concept of "low cost Mutual Funds" is now a reality.

Generally, the tendency is to buy a whole load of Mutual Funds and stick them into one's portfolio. But because of the way these vehicles are structured, you often end up with a lot of duplication/overlap in your holdings. For instance, a Technology-focused Mutual Fund might have Apple (AAPL) as its largest holding. But a large-cap Fund might also have the same. This means you might end up with an unhealthy excess of a single stock if your portfolio had both those Funds in it.

To address this, investment companies like Vanguard offer a diversified 3-Fund Portfolio (more about this tool later!) that can be an ideal Lazy investment. Since the 3 funds are "packaged" to work as a complete portfolio option, it offers better diversification than building a portfolio by choosing individual Funds.

The downside (there always has to be at least one, we suppose) is that such multi-fund portfolio builders often have a minimum amount of investment required for each fund. In the case of the Vanguard 3-Fund Portfolio, the minimum per fund is $3,000. And that might make it an unrealistic Lazy investment option for most beginners.

To address that deficiency, most Fund Management companies offer parallel, low-cost, lower minimal investment ETF (more on ETFs shortly) options that match most of their Mutual Funds.

ii) Index Funds:

While Index Funds look and feel the same as Mutual Funds (in fact, they may also be called Index Mutual Funds), they do have some fundamental differences:

- They are lower-cost cousins to Mutual Funds
- Unlike traditional Mutual Funds, they are (usually) not actively managed
- They are designed to follow or mimic their benchmarks and not try and beat them

- They are built not on the basis of stock picking individual stocks, but instead track an entire universe of stocks through exposure to the whole index (like S&P 500 or DJIA)

As a Lazy investors tool, Index Funds don't offer speculation of stocks. There is no manager that actively picks or drops a stock from the fund. Since Index Funds are passively managed (though active versions are now being made available), they end up being relatively cheaper (in terms of expenses) than their higher-cost Mutual Fund cousins.

On the average, Index Funds (usually) outperform Mutual Funds over the longer term (5, 10, 15+ years). That's because they tend to be more broadly diversified (entire market versus specific stocks) than Mutual Funds, and they don't incur all of the research and transaction fees that come with oft-traded Mutual Funds.

Of course, there are those that will vigorously dispute the fact that actively managed funds often tend to (over the long term) lag behind their benchmark. Cold hard facts are the only way to silence them:

A comparison of how many actively managed funds have **NOT** managed to beat their indices over 1, 3 and 5-years is proof that "active" does NOT = better returns.

And if you still need convincing that Index Funds are right for you, don't take our word. Listen to what the world's most famous investor (a.k.a. "The Oracle of Omaha") says about them:

"I'd rather be certain of a good return than hopeful of a great one. — Most investors are better off putting their money in low-cost index funds." - **Warren Buffett**

So, the next time your Financial Advisor "strongly advises" you to jump into something active, simply show him/her a copy of this chart and yell:

"In your face!"

iii) Exchange Traded Funds (ETFs)

We're sure that you've heard the age-old maxim: "If you can't beat 'em, join 'em!"?

Well, that about sums up how ETF's came into being. You see, over the past 8 to 10 years or so, the real truth about Mutual Funds has been dawning upon many investors who are too lazy to start picking stocks themselves. This select group of investors thought: "Hmm...instead of picking one or two stocks, why don't we just own a basket of them through a Mutual Fund?"

All very well. But as time went by, investors started learning about:

- The real cost of owning these instruments
- The fact that most actively managed Funds weren't doing what they promised - beating their indices
- The fact that "owning a basket" didn't necessarily give them exposure to the entire index

And the more they learned, the more they started questioning: Why pay all those costs if the Funds active managers can't consistently deliver? And that's when some very astute Fund Management companies decided to do something about offering lower-cost investment products for the Lazy investor. This realization lead to the creation of passively (Lazy) managed index ETFs, which were instruments that:

- Were built to be more cost effective than Mutual Funds and many traditional Index Funds
- Were designed to better protect investors from the impact of Capital Gains taxes
- Did not need to be actively traded, like their Mutual Fund cousins
- Could be priced on an ongoing basis (minute-by-minute, daily) in the markets, unlike Mutual Funds whose price is only calculated at the end of a trading day

The Financial Industry Regulatory Authority (FINRA), the US body tasked to oversee investment companies and their practices, did an interesting comparison on fees of Mutual Funds versus their ETF cousins.

So when the decision comes down to: 'Are you receiving value for money (i.e. given the understanding that actively managed funds aren't a guarantee for stellar returns!)?', then the choice is really simple enough to make - isn't it?

I can tell that you like this...so let's make it slightly more interesting, shall we?

Given that a company (for example - Vanguard) offers both a Mutual Fund as well as a corresponding ETF, does it matter which one you should choose? The answer is: Choose the laziest of the investments!

In the above case, the passive ETF (VV) from Vanguard does much better than its passively managed Index Mutual Fund (VLACX) over a 4-year period. The moral of the story, therefore, is, given that all things are equal, **the laziest of investments will always serve you better than an actively managed one**. And a passively managed ETF does far better than actively managed Mutual funds.

Having said that however, we must remember that ETFs and Mutual Funds both have their place in well diversified portfolios; it's just a matter of choosing the right instruments for your comfort levels.

iv) Dividend Reinvestment Plans (DRIPs)

So, you've got some investments in your portfolio - Index Funds, ETFs Mutual Funds, but you are just too lazy to watch them on a day-to-day, month-to month basis. Sure, the respective fund managers "do their thing" with the overall fund (buy, sell, rebalance), but what about your own portfolio - who is looking after it?

That's where a neat little Lazy investment trick called Dividend Reinvestment Plans (DRIPs) comes in. Contrary to their name however, DRIPs aren't just restricted to dividends. Other forms of cash returns (including ETF distributions and Return of Capital) can be mobilized in DRIP programs.

Essentially, what a DRIP is telling your portfolio to do is:

- Collect all those dividends and distributions, and **automatically** use the proceeds to buy more of the same investment vehicles

The result is a neat little repeated investment plan that doesn't need any further monitoring. Your DRIP is the ultimate Lazy "set it and forget it" investment plan. Each distribution period, the proceeds received from your investment will be automatically re-invested into the instruments from which those proceeds come from.

In most cases, DRIPs offer more than simple, Lazy, carefree investment. They offer real financial benefits to members of the plan:

- Usually, units of the investment (Stock, Mutual Fund, Index Fund or ETF) are purchased commission-free through DRIPs. Imagine the savings you can accumulate over time...
- In a majority of cases, DRIP-purchased units are offered at a discount. For instance, if a particular Stock or Mutual Fund is trading at $20 per unit, using a DRIP to purchase it may cost you $19.95 per unit. Imagine how much that will save you over a thousand units...
- By and large, Stocks, Mutual Funds and Index Funds have to be purchased in whole units. So, if you plan on buying a unit of a fund that costs $500 a pop, you will only be able to buy 1 unit with a $700 investment. The remaining $200 will sit there until you add another $300 to buy a second unit. Not so with DRIPs. They allow the purchase of fractional units, which means your money (even if it is $2), doesn't sit idle. It's fully invested, earning you additional dividends and distributions.
- DRIPs are ideal ways to take advantage of the unique concept called dollar cost averaging - where you continually buy a particular Fund (or stock) at predetermined times, and over time, your cost of ownership is likely to be much lower than the prevailing cost. Thereby, you'll gain a healthy capital appreciation in the process.

So, by simply enrolling into a DRIP program, you can take advantage of the Lazy investor's ultimate play: Sit back, relax, and watch your investment do its thing!

v) Employer Investment Plans (EIPs)

If you are lucky enough to be employed at a company that offers EIPs, you would be well advised to take full advantage of it. This is yet another tool in the Lazy Investors' tool kit that many are not aware they have.

Here's how it works:

- Every pay period, a certain percentage of your paycheck is deducted (directly at source)
- The proceeds are usually held in trust, and used to purchase stock, usually (but not necessarily so) of the employing company
- The company then matches the amount deducted from your paycheque, and adds an equivalent (or predetermined percentage) amount to your investment portfolio
- So, for example, if you had $50 deducted from your pay, the company will add another $50, and you'd receive $100 (or whatever the employer contribution amount is at your company) worth of company stock (or applicable investment)

EIPs are a great Lazy investment tool because they don't require any portfolio management or rebalancing or monitoring on your part. Paycheck after paycheck, you'll watch your holdings of the company's' stock (or applicable investment) increase as the Plan managers purchase the stock on your behalf.

Usually, there is a management fee charged for executing the transactions in the EIP, but those are way below what you'd have to pay were you to buy your employers stock through your broker or your discount brokerage account. And in the process, EIPs:

- Provide employees a truly lazy option to investing for their retirement (or other objective)
- Give employees "free money" from the employer that otherwise would not have been available
- Create a low-cost investment vehicle that employees can use for truly risk free investing. Why? Because the investment will need to drop a minimum of 50% (if that's the employer matching ratio) before it is considered a loss-making investment. And that's a risk worth taking!

Unfortunately, not every employer offers EIPs, and many employees who do work for companies offering them aren't taking full advantage of this "free money" offer from employers.

vi) Target Date Funds/ETFs

Over the past few years, a renewed focus is being put on investors needing a carefree way to plan for their retirement. Target Date investments (Mutual Funds and ETFs) are a new way for Lazy investors to plan for a targeted retirement date. How these work is really simple:

- Fund companies offer funds with differing investment time horizons - 5 years, 10 years, 15 years etc.
- Periodically, as/when a targeted date comes closer to fruition, the longer-duration investments are converted into shorter-duration ones
- For example, a 15-year target date investment made today will automatically be converted into a 10-year fund after 5 years of purchasing it (the 15-year vehicle).
- Similarly, 5 years after you invest in a 10-year Fund, your investments will automatically be rolled into a 5-year fund

This is an ideal Lazy investment tool. Why? Because investors will never have to keep track of maturity dates. As long as you know when (approximately) your retirement is likely to occur, you can select a product and forget about it. The fund managers will automatically take care of the rollover into shorter duration investments as the clock ticks by.

In addition to being a lazy investor's friend, from a time-horizon monitoring stand point, there is one other crucial advantage to using this tool in your lazy portfolio:

- The types of investments made in these instruments mirror what typical investment advice suggests: The longer out your retirement horizon is, the more risk you can take. The nearer the impending retirement date is, the less riskier your investments should become

The rationale behind this is simple: If riskier investments (i.e. Stocks/Equities) falter, they will have a longer runway to rebound. And that's why longer-term target date funds/ETFs invest more of their portfolios in stocks/equities, and less in fixed income: e.g. 70%-30%. As the retirement horizon shrinks, the mix of riskier versus safe investments change: say 60%-40% for a retirement that's 10 years out, 50%-50% for a 5-year retirement plan, and 70%-30% for a 2 to 3 year retirement plan.

vii) Laddered GICs/CDs

Portfolio planning experts always advise investors, Lazy ones or not, to hold some percentage of their savings in fixed income vehicles. Certificates of Deposits (CDs) or Guaranteed Income Certificates (GICs) are one way to do just that. However, over the past several years, financial institutions have come up with a great Lazy Investor offering featuring GICs/CDs.

The tool is called Laddered GICs/CDs, and is constructed using a "step" approach for investing in fixed income certificates.

Here's how these work:

- Say you have $5,000 to allocate to the fixed income part of your portfolio
- Then, you buy a 5-year Laddered investment with that amount
- The investment will be divided into 5 instalments, each worth $1,000 in value
- Each of the $1,000 will be invested in fixed-term, fixed-income deposits ranging from 1 to 5 years
- After Year 1, the $1,000 will be re-invested into a 5-year maturity fixed income vehicle, thereby restoring your 1 to 5 year "ladder"
- This goes on each year as one of the $1,000 investments come due, giving you a perpetual 5-year ladder in fixed investments

The advantage of Laddering is that, once you decide on how your ladder is to be built, you never need to worry about re-balancing or re-scheduling it.

- Most ladder providers offer options for auto-renewal, along with flexible terms to renew
- You can choose to renew just the principle, or both principle as well as accumulated interest
- Or you may choose to disband the ladder all together after it has run its original course

For Lazy investors who are living off interest, choosing to have the interest deposited into a checking account while continuing with the ladder perpetually, might be an attractive carefree investing idea.

c) Limitations

Lazy Investing is a great idea for investors who:

- Lack the investment knowledge to stay on top of fast-moving market conditions
- Don't have the time to spend continually monitoring, rebalancing and modifying their portfolios
- Lack the patience required of active portfolio management strategies

The idea is to "set it and forget it". However, being a Lazy investor also means there are certain limitations to this strategy. I can hear you guys and gals go: "Uh oh...here it comes!". Well, no investment style is perfect, and Lazy Investing is no exception. However, as you will see, the "limitations" aren't really all that bad. And for each of these limitations, there are easy workarounds:

- While investors can definitely "set it and forget it", Lazy investments should not be totally ignored. Periodically, it would be prudent to take a peek at how things are going. At that time, should the need arise, finer adjustments may be necessary. However, such adjustments are likely to be far less than if you pursue an active investment strategy
- Lazy does not equal "ignorant". Since Lazy investors are usually DIY (do-it-yourself) investors, there is a need to do some upfront diligence before choosing where to invest. While the same might be said about other investment styles, DIY approaches often mean the individual investor (and not a Broker/Advisor) is ultimately responsible for all decisions
- Lazy investing is contrary to individual stock picking. So, if you see a particular Lazy product (Index Fund, ETF) that fits well with your investment thesis, you'll have to "take it all -

or leave it all!" There is no room to say, "I'll take this ETF, plus include these 2 stocks that are not in it". You can't be selective, like you can when relying on individual stock picks. As an alternate, you may want to open a discount brokerage account if you want to dabble in a few choice stocks that aren't available in your Lazy portfolio

- And speaking of choice, you may also not have much choice when it comes to a Lazy Portfolio, because some 401(k) plan managers might not offer them. However, shopping around for alternates always pays. For instance, if a particular type of Treasury index funds isn't offered in retirement plans, use an alternate: invest 50% in a tax-free Treasury fund (instead of Treasury index funds).

All in all, given that Lazy Portfolios are easy creation, low-maintenance ways for investors to build a portfolio, the limitations discussed above shouldn't detract anyone from embracing them.

WHO IS LAZY INVESTING RIGHT FOR?

Now that you've got a closer look at what Lazy Investing is all about, and especially some of its limitations, you may be right in asking: "So, who should really embrace Lazy Investing?" You are probably taking a closer look at your own investments and wondering: "Is Lazy Investing really for me?"

Well, before we start looking at the profile of the ideal Lazy Investor, let's pause for a minute and do a quick recap of WHY investors like the Lazy Investing thesis:

- Because it gives them the flexibility to not have to constantly "mess" with their portfolios
- Because it won't eat away at their money with trading fees, broker fees, and a hundred other little fees that really add up
- Because it offers them the advantage of not having to be an expert in every investment they own
- Because it gives them a low-cost option to invest for the long run

All of this might sound like beating a dead horse, but this horse still has some life in it, so we're going to beat it just a bit more to highlight who lazy investing is right for:

a) Everyone!

The term "Lazy Investment" is really a misnomer. When active investors hear about anything "lazy", they may immediately tune out of the discussion. That would be a mistake.

Despite the title, Lazy Investments are for EVERYONE - regardless of the level of investment knowledge, or the time they spend monitoring or managing their investments. Why? Because they offer another viable investment alternate (to active investment) that EVERYONE should at least consider - if not wholeheartedly embrace.

The discussions that we've had so far, including all of the lovely graphs and tables that were shared with you earlier, should have convinced you that not all actively managed portfolios perform as designed. In fact, a large number of them fail to do so, quite spectacularly. So, given that not EVERYONE's actively managed portfolio will see them through to retirement, what should they be doing about it NOW?

And the answer is (drum roll please...): Consider allocating at least a portion of their retirement savings to a Lazy Portfolio. Worst case scenario: Your Lazy Portfolio will deliver returns in line with the indices they track, which - as we have seen through statistical evidence - will offer pretty decent returns. Best case scenario: Based on all the evidence we've shared with you, your Lazy Portfolio is more than likely to outperform your actively managed investments.

In short, everyone should consider Lazy Investments, even if it's not the primary form of investing they adopt.

b) 'SAFE' Retirement Planners

Lazy Investments are especially suited for investors looking for a "safe" bet for their retirements. Why? Because there is no high-risk stock picking involved, and because of the inherently conservative way most of these investments are structured.

Retirement planning is often a long-term goal, and needs foresight and good planning. If you are in the younger-to-prime of your life (early 20's or 30's), you might be able to take some risk with more volatile investment approaches. Should you encounter several years of market turbulence, your lengthy investment time horizon (35-45 years) allows greater latitude for risk taking. With that many years of staying in the market, there is a high degree of probability that you will recoup most (if not all) of your losses.

But individuals nearing retirement, say 3 to 5 years from today, can't afford to risk a few bad market years that could wipe out hard earned gains from a decade or more of savings. Betting on a few "hot stocks" could spell disaster! However, the right mix of Lazy Investments is a great tool when you are planning for an imminent retirement.

But Lazy Investing isn't just a safe way to invest when retirement is imminent. Even if you are a long way from retiring, and don't want to risk it all to an actively managed portfolio, you could allocate a certain portion of your retirement savings to the safer Lazy Portfolio, while investing the rest in an active portfolio.

The operative word here is "safe" retirement. And that's what Lazy Portfolios are designed to provide!

c) Diversification Seekers

Okay, I've said it a thousand times...but I'll say it just once more:

Lazy Investment isn't about doing "hot stock picking"!

If you would have learned one thing from this book so far, it should have been that Lazy Investors hate micromanaging their portfolios. They hate building spreadsheet models that will tell them what the Price/Earnings (PE) Ratio or Price/Book Value of a "great stock" is. They hate looking at company Balance Sheets and P&L Statements to figure out which company is profitable, so they can invest in its stock. Well, maybe they don't *hate* it, necessarily, but they certainly realize that doing all of that work won't increase their chances of successfully predicting how a stock will move in the future.

At its very heart, Lazy Investing is about making life easy for ordinary investors. So instead of spinning wheels fast and furiously, trading stocks very frequently (and losing money to fees in the process), Lazy Investors use diversification as a way to hedge themselves against any downturns in the market.

By contrast, active managers prefer to make things more complex than they really are - and where does that leave your portfolio?

- You may own half a dozen or so stocks in one particular sector
- You might own a handful of stocks on one particular index
- You may even get to own a few stocks that are doing extremely well this week!

But even as an active manager, you'll be hard pressed to hold, monitor and track more than 20 to 30 stocks at any given time. And that means your portfolio will be hugely under diversified - which is one of the major risks that portfolio managers tend to avoid.

So how can you mitigate the risk of under diversification? You got it (drum roll again...!): It's by owning a much broader, well diversified basket of stocks through a lazy portfolio comprising ETF's or Index Funds.

Since ETFs and Index Funds hold many more individual stocks than individual portfolio holders can, a Lazy portfolio will offer much greater diversification than you would get holding 20 or 30 stocks. The objective of owning ETFs and Index Funds with large diversified holdings comes from the fact that:

- Since many Lazy investors, such as yourself, are investing in them, there is a larger pool of investable cash to play with. This gives fund managers the advantage of volume and size - something that a small portfolio with 20 or 30 stocks lacks
- Depending on the product you invest in, you could own the entire Index, or broad segments of it
- In bad times, it is usually certain sectors that fall, while others rise. By holding more than just 20 or 30 stocks (in some instances you could be holding over 200 individual equities in an ETF or Index Fund!), the downside of your portfolio will be more than mitigated by its up side
- By way of an example: If only 2 of your 20 stocks take a hit during particularly volatile trading sessions, it will impact 10% of your holdings. By contrast, those same 2 stocks will only represent 1% of your 200-stock ETF or Index Fund
- Because of your broad diversification, you'll be much better protected than had you cherry picked the 20 or 30 stocks to begin with

So if you are looking for a well-diversified group of investments, then you can get it with a Lazy Portfolio, and not by building your own through individual stock picks.

d) Cost Conscious Investors

Okay...here we go again, talking about costs!

But the reason why we are revisiting the topic of costs is because it is so critically important. Through the evidence we have presented in previous sections of this book, it should be clear to you that costs can actually make or break your retirement dreams.

Remember the example we discussed back in Section 3, where a 1.25% cost eroded almost 51% of an actively managed portfolio? Well, to put things in perspective, that's like going out and spending $300,000 to buy a 2-bedroom house, only to find that you own just a single bedroom, while your Realtor owns the other!

Would you be comfortable making a deal as harsh as that? You don't even need to answer - I know exactly what you're going to say.

Well, investment costs work the same way. But because the costs are charged in small doses, and over an extended period (in our example it was spread over 50 years), they do not immediately raise red flags. Why? Because that's how they were designed! Additionally, because the Mutual Fund companies don't want those red flags raised, they wrap the "true costs" deep inside fine print.

Still not convinced about the "cost thing" - are you? Well, let's look at costs from the point of view of two REAL investment types, shall we?

A "typical" Mutual Fund (with an Income/Growth profile) will have an expense ratio of approximately 1.29%. So, on an investment of $10,000, over the course of roughly 10 years you'll have paid $1,885 to the fund company.

Now contrast that with a low-cost Indexed fund - these are available at MER's as low as 0.12%. For the equivalent investment, and the same time horizon, you'll only pay $154 in expenses. That's a difference of over $1,725! And when you factor compounding into the equation, that difference grows even more significant!

That's why Lazy Investing has been designed for cost conscious investors who are aware of the true costs of active investing. Using low-cost investment vehicles, that don't require frequent management, the Lazy Portfolio will outperform any actively managed portfolio in the long run. And that's what attracts cost conscious investors to it!

THE ULTIMATE LAZY INVESTMENT PORTFOLIO

Congratulations...you're now ready to explore some REAL Lazy Investment portfolios with us. I hear many of you sigh: It's about time! And we couldn't agree with you more. So we'll get right on with it. But before we do, let's take a few minutes to explain some underlying principles of building a Lazy Portfolio.

- **Objective:** Like any portfolio that you construct, the objective for building your Lazy Portfolio must be clear. We've talked a lot about investing for retirement in this book. But not every investment objective is about retirement planning - though it does seem to be the predominant theme. But it could equally be to save for a home, children's education, a family vacation.
  Lazy Investors must have clarity in mind about the objectives for building the portfolio, because the types of lazy investing building blocks to use will depend on those goals and objectives.

- **Time Horizon:** Lazy Portfolios are not for short-term investors. If you have a 3 to 6 month time horizon to make some quick money, then a Lazy Portfolio is not your vehicle of choice. Perhaps a discount brokerage trading account might do you well. Some actively managed portfolios might also provide better short-term returns. Ideally, a Lazy Portfolio should look at an investment horizon of at least 3 to 5+ years.

- **Risk aversion:** As we've said time and again, Lazy Portfolios are not about risking it all for big gains. Lazy Portfolios therefore use relatively low-risk, low-cost investment instruments that tend to outperform their more risky peers over the long term. If you are a high risk seeking investor, you may not like the slow-and-steady progress of a Lazy Portfolio.

- **Patience:** Lazy Portfolios are built on, and reward, patience. What that means is that, over a 5 to 10 year investment horizon, expect to have several quarters or even a few years of bad performance. But if you have patience and stay the course with your Lazy Portfolio, despite the occasional bumps in the road, you will be rewarded.

- **Asset mix:** Ultimately, no one (no, not even us) can tell YOU what your asset mix should be when constructing a Lazy Portfolio. But to build it, you must have a clear idea of what percentage you need to allocate to Equities and Fixed Income (e.g. Bonds).

Now, having got that off our plate, let's take a closer look at some Lazy Portfolio options out there, shall we?

a) 3-Fund Portfolio

One of the simplest ways to construct a Lazy Portfolio is by using a 3-Fund approach. Generally, a 3-Fund Portfolio uses three Index Funds to create it:

- A total-market Domestic equity fund
- A total-market International equity fund; and
- A total-market Bond index fund

As can be seen, with just these 3 funds, Lazy Investors can participate in three key aspects of diversification - domestic and international stocks, and fixed income (Bonds). And that's the kind of simplicity that Lazy Portfolio's are known for.

3-Fund Portfolios don't require investors to indulge in any additional slicing and dicing of their portfolios. You won't need to study volatility charts or Candlestick diagrams of individual Stocks or Bonds. That's like searching for 3 needles in 3 proverbial haystacks. Instead, you just go ahead and buy all three haystacks using the 3-Fund Portfolio.

Sample 3-Fund Portfolios

A number of fund managers offer great individual funds that investors can quickly use to create 3-Fund Portfolios of their own. Some worth considering are:

The Vanguard offerings:

- Vanguard Total Stock Market Index Fund (VTSMX)
- Vanguard Total International Stock Index Fund (VGTSX)
- Vanguard Total Bond Market Fund (VBMFX)

The Fidelity Choice:

- Fidelity Spartan Total Market Index Fund (FSTMX)
- Fidelity Spartan Global ex U.S. Index Fund (FSGDX)
- Fidelity Spartan U. S. Bond Index Fund (FBIDX)

Charles Schwab's' options:

- Schwab Total Stock Market Index (SWTSX)
- Schwab International Index (SWISX)
- Schwab Total Bond Market (SWLBX)

Individual Lazy Investors can start off with a conservative mix of each of these 3 ingredients, and then, over time, you can rebalance your portfolio to match your desired levels of exposure to each class.

i) ETF-based:

We've talked a lot in previous segments of this book, about how efficient ETF's are as a Lazy Investment vehicle. For those Lazy investors who prefer ETF's to Index or Mutual funds, there are a number of individual ETF's that can be used as building blocks to pull together a Lazy 3-ETF Portfolio.

While investing in ETFs might offer many of the same advantages as were discussed for Index Funds above, they may offer greater cost advantage than Index or Mutual Funds. Additionally, since some ETFs might provide their distributions in the form of "Return of Capital", ETF's may even provide slight (at least in the near-term) tax efficiencies over their Index or Mutual Fund cousins.

Sample 3-ETF Portfolios

The following ETF's might be worth considering when deciding to build a 3-ETF Lazy Portfolio:

T.Rowe Price offerings:

- T.Rowe Price offers a range of ETF's including iShares, QQQ, SPDRs, DIA and HOLDRs

Vanguard offerings:

- Vanguard Total Stock Market ETF (VTI)
- Vanguard Total International Stock ETF (VXUS)
- Vanguard Total Bond Market ETF (BND)

Fidelity offerings:

- Fidelity Nasdaq Composite Index (ONEQ)
- Fidelity MSCI-based Sector ETF's, including (FDIS), or (FSTA) or (FNCL) or (FIDU)
- Fidelity Total Bond ETF (FBND)

While the above list of ETF's has been organized by sponsor (e.g. T.Rowe Price, Vanguard or Fidelity), there's nothing to stop a Lazy Investor to mix/match the list of 3 ETF's to construct their individual Lazy Portfolios. For instance, a valid 3-ETF portfolio might easily include POMIX (T.Rowe), VXUS (Vanguard) and FBIDX (Fidelity).

The bottom line is, if you feel comfortable with a certain ETF sponsor, or a particular ETF they offer (versus similar products offered by other sponsors), you should not hesitate to consider adding it to your portfolio. It goes without saying though, before making your final decision, considerations such as Fees, Track record and reputation should be evaluated.

b) Is there magic in 3? The 2-Holdings Portfolio

The simple answer is: NO!

There is really no magic in deciding to go with a 3-holding portfolio (more about this later). However, at this point it is sufficient to note that the number of holdings depend entirely on one's comfort level. For instance, there are products out there that are merged versions of "Market" and "Bond" Funds/ETFs. Such products allow Lazy Investors the option to get Market and Bond exposure by owning just a single investment vehicle.

If you decide to go the "merged" route and own a combination Market/Bond product, then the only other thing left would be to pick an International stock offering, and you should have a well constructed 2-Fund Lazy portfolio.

Take the T. Rowe Price Balanced Mutual Fund (RPBAX) for instance. It has a rough asset allocation of:

- 45% Domestic Stocks
- 10% Domestic Bonds
- 21% Foreign Stocks
- 4% Foreign Bonds

To compliment RPBAX, a Lazy Investor could search for a product that has greater International Stock and Foreign Bond exposure, and that would produce a well-rounded 2-Fund Lazy Portfolio.

Another example of creating a 2-Fund Lazy Portfolio might involve using the Vanguard Balanced Index Fund (VBIAX), which invests 60% in the overall U.S stock market, and 40% in a broad based bond index. To round this up and fold it into a 2-Fund Lazy Portfolio, all that's needed is to find an International Stock fund (or ETF) of your liking and you should be good to go.

c) Couch Potato Portfolio:

While not truly the originator of the concept of low-cost investing, a contributing writer and personal finance expert at the Dallas Morning News, Scott Burns, pioneered the Couch Potato Portfolio. Since then, these have become an industry standard for all lazy investors, upon which to model their portfolios.

As it was originally designed, Burns' vision of the Couch Potato Portfolio involved investing their total pool of money half-and-half into:

- A index fund from the S&P 500 Index; and
- Investing the remaining 50% in the Shearson/Lehman Intermediate Bond Index

As his vehicles of choice, Burns chose the following 2 Vanguard products to construct his initial Couch Potato Portfolio:

- 50%: Vanguard 500 Index (VFINX)
- 50%: Vanguard Total Bond Fund Index (VBMFX)

The idea behind structuring this portfolio the way it is, was to provide Lazy investors equal exposure to both equities and fixed income investments. Burns also suggested that, depending upon one's risk tolerance, one could structure their holdings into what he called a "sophisticated Couch Potato Portfolio". This sophistication would see investors expose 75% of their holdings to VFINX (equities) and 25% to VBMFX (fixed income).

It goes without saying however, that experimentation with "sophistication" would only suite more younger Lazy investors, since they would typically have a longer time horizon for recovery, should there be a drastic market correction.

Lazy investors who are approaching retirement, or already retired, could further change their investment mix with a greater bias (75%) to fixed income (VBMFX) and lesser (25%) towards equities VFINX.

d) Couch Potato Variants:

The popularity of the Burns Couch Potato Portfolio fueled greater interest in the Lazy investing approach, and got more mainstream investment professionals into thinking about their own versions of the Couch Potato portfolios.

While each of the above portfolios has dramatically different asset mixes, they are predominantly based on Index investment products from Vanguard - the pioneer of low-cost products for DIY investors. However, Lazy Investing is not just the domain of Vanguard, as products from a number of fund managers can easily be used to quickly build a Lazy Couch-Potato-based portfolio.

The above is yet another example of a well diversified portfolio that uses none of the Vanguard products. Instead, this one is created from products mainly available from iShares and Fidelity. The underlying themes though, of any of these Lazy/Couch-Potato and variant portfolios, are:

- They are based on low-cost products
- They rely heavily on ETFs and Index Funds
- They offer exceptional diversity in construction
- They are low-maintenance, and require only periodic re-balancing

And for investors who are too lazy to organize their lives around their investments, these and other Couch-Potato variant portfolios are ideal long-term investment tools.

e) Some Other Lazy Portfolio Considerations

So, now you know enough about Lazy investing to understand that labelling this kind of investing "lazy" is actually a misnomer.

While you (the holder of the portfolio) may enjoy a leisurely peek, now and again, at your investments, the investments themselves are working feverishly on your behalf. In fact, given that lazy investments outperform many actively managed ones, some may argue they work even harder than their actively-managed peers!

Be that as it may, no discussion on building lazy portfolios would be complete without mentioning a few hallmarks about the investor's mental attitude and approach.

i) Invest-and-Forget Approach:

We've already talked about the "laid back" approach that Lazy investors need to cultivate in order to be good at this particular style of investing. What this means is that you refrain from tinkering, tampering, or tweaking your portfolio too often. Having said that however, does that mean you need to take a "laid back" approach when building such portfolios too?

Absolutely, definitely, totally NOT!

In this context, "Lazy" does not equal callous or haphazard. In fact, the building blocks of every lazy portfolio require as much diligence to put together as any of their actively managed peers. But once the investment decisions have been made - after careful consideration of course - Lazy Portfolios should be forgotten. Give them room to "do their thing" and show you their magic.

And that's the "invest-and-forget" approach required to get the best out of a Lazy Portfolio!

ii) Non-Trading Mentality:

So, why did you pick the Turtle over the Hare in the first place? Because you wanted to win at a leisurely pace, and didn't want to jump in and out the racecourse, that's why!

It's the same with Lazy Portfolios. To be successful at lazy investing, investors should forget the "Buy low", "Sell high" mentality.

Understand that trading costs money. And money spent on trades, over time, will erode whatever gains a Lazy Portfolio might have accumulated for you. Even though a particular investment might be riding high on a wave of volatility, it behoves Lazy Investors to resist the temptation of "cashing in" and waiting until the next dip to get back in.

Whenever you are tempted to do a quick trade, just think of the oft-repeated saying:

It's time in the market - and not timing the market - that'll get you stellar returns!"

And that's the kind of mentality that Lazy Investors must cultivate!

iii) Self-Building Approach:

One of the best tools in the Lazy Investors toolbox is the automatic building approach. And these come in two main forms:

- **Pre-approved Investing Plans (PIPs):** Which are automatic investments of a predetermined amount, at a predetermined frequency, made into the portfolio. Once set, these designated amounts are automatically withdrawn (from a Checking or Saving account), and used to purchase additional units of Lazy investments.
- **Dividend/distribution Reinvestments (DRIPs):** We've already spoken at length about this tool previously. Here, in the context of self-building lazy portfolios, we'd like to emphasize that DRIPs can be used as a self-contained portfolio building mechanism. The funds generated in DRIPs

come from within the portfolio, and not externally from a Checking or Savings account; and they are used within the portfolio as well.

Since both these tools are "set and forget" vehicles, a Lazy Investor does not need to take any further action to replenish the Lazy Portfolio with new investment. It all happens automatically, with a minimum of administration and practically no maintenance costs.

iv) The Insulation Effect:

Lazy Portfolios are well insulated from the volatility and turbulence of short-term market gyrations. But that happens only because investors choose an appropriate blend of instruments as their asset mix. For instance, in a typical Lazy Portfolio, you are invested in:
- A U.S. stock index
- An International stock index
- A bond index

or some variations of these asset classes. As a result, the Lazy Portfolio receives the most diversification possible, thereby creating an insulation effect that other portfolios not similarly diversified lack.

f) How Many Holdings Are Good?:

You are obviously looking for an absolute response here. But I'll duck the question and answer: It depends!

"Huh! What kind of an answer is THAT?", I hear you say! Well, it's the best that anyone can give you, without knowing your:

- Investible pot of money
- Investment objectives

- Time Horizon
- Risk Appetite
- Pre-disposition towards ETFs, Mutual Funds, Index Funds
- Preference for Fixed Income versus Equities

...and so on.

But refer back to our discussion on "Is there magic in 3?". If it wasn't made clear then, let's make it clear now: There is no magic number as to how many holdings are good for an ideal Lazy Portfolio. Great Lazy Portfolios can be constructed with as few as 2 holdings, or they may take up to 10 holdings to construct. The choice is yours.

A simple rule to deciding how many holdings are "good", is to ask yourself:

- Do the holdings I have chosen provide me sufficient diversification?
- Are they contributing to a well-balanced portfolio?
- When it comes time to review or rebalance, can I handle this number of holdings and still do justice to my portfolio decisions?

Other than that, one final rule is: Keep it simple!

g) How Should It Be Built?:

I'd like to say "With great care and consideration!" But you may think I'm being flippant. I'm not! When you sit down to construct a Lazy Portfolio, you need to keep an open mind, but you also need to be completely focused on the task at hand.

Here are a few considerations to give when planning a custom-built Lazy Portfolio

i) Consideration #1: A Single Portfolio

Not every investor has $100,000 to start with when building a portfolio. So, if your initial investible sum is relatively small ($3,000 - $5,000), you might want to just want to start with a 50:50 allocation in a 2-Fund portfolio.

If, on the other hand, you have a considerably larger sum to invest ($100,000+), or if your initial small portfolio grows larger, then you might want to mix-and-match by either adding additional holdings to your existing portfolio and rebalancing, or maintaining more than one portfolio.

The beauty of Lazy Investing and building Lazy Portfolios is that there are no hard-and-fact rules. YOU decide what's best, as long as it follows the broad guidelines laid out in the previous sections of this book.

ii) Consideration #2: Split into Sheltered versus Non-Sheltered?:

For some Lazy investors, the protection of their retirement nest egg might be a supreme consideration when deciding how to structure an investment portfolio. Perhaps, for the safety and security they offer, you could consider building your retirement portfolio (401-k) using Lazy building blocks, while maintaining a parallel portfolio of actively-managed investments in a non-retirement portfolio.

As we discussed earlier, another consideration when dealing specifically with retirement accounts, has to be whether Lazy investment products are available for such portfolios.

EPILOGUE

And there we have it: You are now officially a Lazy Investing "guru"!

Forget about all the buzzwords thrown at you by Wall Street-types. Don't listen to your Broker/Advisor about the pitfalls of going it alone. Documented historical returns favor you, the Lazy Investor. In the long run, your portfolio will be:

- Quicker to build
- Simple to manage
- Cheaper to maintain
- More effective in performance

Independent investment sites like Morningstar.com can easily be used to verify your portfolios performance against the category of its peers. Time and time again, it is your holdings that will make the top of the rankings list - guaranteed!

Lest you walk away with the idea that this book was about recommending a particular fund managers products as building blocks for your Lazy Portfolio - IT IS NOT! While we frequently used examples of Vanguard Index Funds and ETFs, we also introduced you to other products, including PowerShares, iShares, Fidelity, T. Rowe Price and many others.

Our primary purpose in producing this book was to dispel the popularly (and erroneously!) held myth that only actively managed portfolios can help you realize your investment dreams. That's far from the truth! Anyone, even someone with not much investing knowledge, can create and manage a Lazy Portfolio. However, it works even better when you take the time to being an informed, educated Lazy Investor. And hopefully this book has put you well on track for that.

We'll leave you with just a few final thoughts:

- The Lazy Investing and Lazy Portfolio building ideas that we introduced here are exactly that: Just ideas. Every individual should make their decisions based on their own unique circumstances

- Not every portfolio idea discussed above is meant for everyone. However, we are more than comfortable emphatically stating: LAZY PORTFOLIOS ARE FOR EVERYONE!

Happy Lazy Investing to you all!

APPENDICES - The Lazy Investors Toolbo

APPENDIX 1 - Are you Lazy?

Use this checklist to help you determine whether Lazy Investing and a Lazy Portfolio is really meant for you.

- You don't have a lot of investment knowledge, and don't wish to start learning a lot about investing either
- You don't have too much time to monitor and manage your investments
- You'd like to invest in something that doesn't cost too much, yet delivers reasonable returns
- You aren't looking for short-term gains, but are really interested in an investment approach that takes the long-term into consideration
- You aren't interested in stock picking
- You don't want to indulge in stock trading

If you have answered "Yes" to all of these questions, then you definitely fit the profile of a Lazy Investor. Congratulations on your "Lazy" designation. You are a winner!

APPENDIX 2 - Kick the tires!

Before deciding to include a particular investment into your Lazy Portfolio, ask yourself these questions:

- Do the asset classes, held inside the investment, match up with your asset class expectation (See Appendix 2 for your Asset Mix preferences)?
- Do you understand all (or a vast majority) of the investments held in the vehicle being considered: What is the investment about? Is it profitable? Is it in line with your ethical beliefs (e.g. Gambling, Tobacco, Arms and ammunition, Manufacturers using Child Labour, Green-themes)?
- Are you comfortable with the geography in which the investments are located?
- What is the track record of the investment managers?
- If the investment (Fund, ETF) has been making money - at what cost is that profit coming (high Fund Fees? Extensive trading costs?)
- Will adding this investment to the Lazy Portfolio you are designing, result in over-diversification or imbalance to your asset mix?
- Is including this particular investment more tax-efficient than other alternates?
- Is this investment available for including in your retirement accounts?

Receiving satisfactory answers to these questions will give you the peace of mind required knowing that this is the right instrument to add to your Lazy Portfolio.

APPENDIX 3 – Should you join an Employer Investment Plan?

Asking yourself these questions will help determine whether it is advantageous for you to join your Employer Investment Plan, or if you are better off staying away from it:

- Some employers may have a minimum employment period requirement, before any employee is eligible to join their plan. Do you even qualify for joining the EIP sponsored by your employer?
- Do you plan to "stick around" for a while with this employer? If you plan on quitting shortly (within the next few months), it may not be worth the while going through the process of enrolling in the EIP
- Do you already save enough (through other savings vehicles) to make joining the EIP irrelevant for you? - Remember to factor in the "free money" when making this comparison
- Can you afford the regular automatic deduction amount from your paycheck required for the EIP? In some cases, the minimum contribution needed for the plan may exceed your affordability threshold. Make sure that you don't default on other important payments (Rent, Mortgage, Children's school fees, Utilities) by joining the EIP
- Does the EIP require you to pay an annual (or monthly) fee? If so, how much will it cost you? Match that cost with the cost of investing somewhere else, but make sure you add the "free money" you get from EIPs into the mix. If it makes sense, stay with the plan, otherwise opt out
- Does the EIP even offer you the kind of Lazy Portfolio building blocks talked about in this book? If your EIP only offers high-cost Mutual Funds, you may be better off staying away. Do the math first!

- Will you receive "free advice" (though you may be paying for it through administration fees!) from the Plan Managers, and will such advice include helping you make the right choice of investments?
- Is there a cost for moving out of the plan? If so, is it acceptable to you - especially if you think you may be leaving the plan (soon/within the foreseeable future)?

If you are satisfied with the responses you receive to these questions, then you probably are better off joining your EIP.

APPENDIX 4 – Lazy Investment options to consider?

Here are a few Lazy Investments to consider when building your Lazy Portfolio:

- Vanguard 500 **Index Fund** Investor Shares (VFINX)
- Vanguard S&P 500 **ETF** (VOO)
- TD Ameritrade SSgA S&P 500 **Index Fund** N Class (SVSPX)
- TD Ameritrade Parnassus Core Equity Fund - Investor Shares (PRBLX)
- Fidelity Asset Manager® 20% (FASIX)
- Fidelity Asset Manager® 40% (FFANX)

APPENDIX 5 – Counting the costs

Here are a few cost elements of a Lazy Investment to consider before you opt for a particular fund when building your Lazy Portfolio:

- Ongoing Fees (also known as the Management Expense Ratio - MER):
    - Management Fee - Also called the 'cost of engaging a Fund Manager', and usually accounts for between 0.5% and 1% of assets under management
    - Administration Costs: These costs cover the day-to-day administrative fees of the fund (Technology, Postage, Legal costs, Record keeping, Compliance)
    - 12B-1 Fee: Usually refers to brokerage commissions and other sales/marketing costs
- Loads:
    - Front End Load Fees: These fees are charged when you purchase the investment
    - Back End Load Fees: Normally, these fees are paid if you sell the fund within a certain window of time - often 3 to 5 years from purchase.
- Transaction Fees:
    - Commissions: If you use a Broker or have a Discount Brokerage account, you will usually be charged a flat fee ($5-$9.99) per Buy and Sell transaction
    - Electronic Exchange Fee: Since your brokerage will use a trading exchange to process your Buy/Sell transaction, you will usually be charged a fee for those services (over and above the commission discussed above)
- Other costs to be aware of:
    - Tax-sheltered accounts: If your Lazy Portfolio is in a tax-sheltered account, you will not need to worry

about the impact of taxes immediately. However, you will have to factor them into the equation when drawing the money out of your account subsequently
- Tax-Free accounts: Since your tax-free Lazy Portfolio is built out of after-tax money, you will never need to factor taxes on such a portfolio
- Taxable Lazy Portfolios: Taxes, such as Income Tax, Capital Gains Tax, Withholding Tax must be factored when making decisions about creating, managing and maintaining a taxable Lazy Portfolio

For more info and further readings, please visit us at
http://www.thelazyinvestors.com

If you've enjoyed this book, PLEASE consider leaving a review and letting others know your thoughts. Thanks!

www.ingramcontent.com/pod-product-compliance
Lightning Source LLC
Chambersburg PA
CBHW071811170526
45167CB00003B/1269